I0606337

INSIDE MLB

ARIZONA DIAMONDBACKS

BY PATRICK DONNELLY

An Imprint of Abdo Publishing
abdobooks.com

abdobooks.com

Published by Abdo Publishing, a division of ABDO, PO Box 398166, Minneapolis, Minnesota 55439.

Printed in the United States of America, North Mankato, Minnesota.
102022
012023

Cover Photo: Rich Schultz/Getty Images Sport/Getty Images
Interior Photos: Christian Petersen/Getty Images Sport/Getty Images, 4; Jeff Carlick/Allsport/Getty Images Sport/Getty Images, 8; Otto Greule Jr./Allsport/Getty Images Sport/Getty Images, 10; John Grieshop/MLB/Getty Images, 12; Owen C. Shaw/Getty Images Sport/Getty Images, 15; Jed Jacobsohn/Allsport/Getty Images Sport/Getty Images, 16, 30; Mike Fiala/AFP/Getty Images, 18; Sporting News/Getty Images, 21, 33; Media News Group/Bay Area News/Getty Images, 22; Barry Gossage/Getty Images Sport/Getty Images, 25; Matthew Stockman/Allsport/Getty Images Sport/Getty Images, 29; Jeff Gross/Getty Images Sport/Getty Images, 34; Scott Cunningham/Getty Images Sport/Getty Images, 37, 38; Norm Hall/Getty Images Sport/Getty Images, 40

Editor: Steph Giedd
Series Designer: Becky Daum

Library of Congress Control Number: 2022940390

Publisher's Cataloging-in-Publication Data

Names: Donnelly, Patrick, author.
Title: Arizona Diamondbacks / by Patrick Donnelly
Description: Minneapolis, Minnesota: Abdo Publishing, 2023 | Series: Inside MLB | Includes online resources and index.
Identifiers: ISBN 9781098290085 (lib. bdg.) | ISBN 9781098275280 (ebook)
Subjects: LCSH: Arizona Diamondbacks (Baseball team)--Juvenile literature. | Baseball teams--Juvenile literature. | Professional sports--Juvenile literature. | Sports franchises--Juvenile literature. | Major League Baseball (Organization)--Juvenile literature.
Classification: DDC 796.35764--dc23

TABLE OF CONTENTS

CHAPTER 1

DIGGING FOR DIAMONDS

Outfielder A. J. Pollock stared out at the mound. The Arizona Diamondbacks batter knew the 2017 National League (NL) wild-card game was on the line. His team was clinging to an 8–7 lead over the Colorado Rockies in the bottom of the eighth inning. Arizona had runners on second and third base with two outs. A base hit by Pollock would drive in some runs and give Arizona some breathing room against the high-powered Rockies. And a hit could help keep a great season from ending too soon for Arizona.

The Diamondbacks had jumped out to an early 6–0 lead at Chase Field in Phoenix. But the Rockies fought back. By the

Diamondbacks outfielder A. J. Pollock reacts after hitting a double during the NL wild-card game on October 4, 2017.

bottom of the eighth inning, Arizona's lead had been trimmed to one run.

Pollock dug in his heels in the batter's box. Veteran Rockies reliever Greg Holland had gotten ahead of him in the count, with one ball and two strikes. Next Holland threw a slider. The pitch hung over the outside corner. Pollock drove it the opposite way, splitting the outfielders and one-hopping the wall in right center. Both runners scored. Pollock raced as fast as he could around the bases. Finally, he slid into third base with a triple.

The home crowd roared. The Diamondbacks had taken a three-run lead. That proved to be more than enough. Arizona held on for an 11–8 victory and kept its season going. The Diamondbacks advanced to the NL Division Series (NLDS), where they would face the Los Angeles Dodgers in a best-of-five showdown. It would prove to be a tough task against the best team in the major leagues. But for one night, the Diamondbacks and their fans could dream big dreams and hope they could add another World Series trophy to their collection.

THE FIRST YEAR

Major League Baseball (MLB) has had a presence in Arizona since the 1940s. But Arizonans didn't have a team to call their own for another 50 years. Instead, Arizona was home to spring training for many teams.

For years most MLB teams held spring training in Florida. But Cleveland owner Bill Veeck didn't want his Black players to be discriminated against in the segregated Deep South. With its warm weather and hot mineral springs, Arizona seemed like a logical fit for a training site. Cleveland started training in Phoenix in 1947. Eventually, others agreed with Veeck. By 2022, 15 teams—or half of all MLB clubs—trained in Arizona as members of the Cactus League.

However, those teams all packed up and left by early April, before the Arizona weather turned brutally hot. Even though Phoenix was a fast-growing city that had landed other major league sports teams, few embraced the idea of playing an outdoor sport in Arizona summers.

A NICKNAME WITH BITE

Fans were given a chance to vote on the team nickname. Coyotes, Diamondbacks, Phoenix, Rattlers, and Scorpions were among the final options. Jerry Colangelo settled on Diamondbacks, a type of rattlesnake native to the region.

The world of major league sports continued to grow, however. And after a decade and a half of stability, MLB decided to expand in the early 1990s. New teams began playing in Miami and Denver in 1993. In 1995 two more cities

The Diamondbacks' first manager, Buck Showalter, looks on as his team plays in a spring training game. In 1999 he led the Diamondbacks to 100 wins in their second season.

were selected as new major league sites—Tampa-St. Petersburg, Florida, and Phoenix.

Jerry Colangelo, owner of the Phoenix Suns of the National Basketball Association (NBA), led the group that was granted the Phoenix expansion team. Their bid had one important requirement. The new owners promised to build a covered stadium to keep players and fans comfortable in the punishing summer weather. Bank One Ballpark was built with a retractable roof. This allowed games to be played with the roof open in nice weather.

Buck Showalter was just 39 years old when Colangelo hired him to manage the Diamondbacks in 1995—two years before their first game. Showalter was a career minor leaguer who had a proven track record as a major league manager, even though he was still younger than some of his players. Showalter had managed the New York Yankees the previous four seasons. And in 1995, he had guided them to the playoffs for the first time in 14 years.

When Showalter arrived in Phoenix, he was given the freedom to craft a team to be just the way he wanted it. Most managers help decide which players will make up the team's roster. Showalter's influence extended to the design of the team's uniforms, the layout of the new spring training complex, the size of the players' lockers, and even the inclusion of a strip of dirt between the pitcher's mound and home plate. This was a callback to the traditional look of classic baseball fields.

BUILDING A ROSTER

The bulk of the first Diamondbacks roster came from an expansion draft held after the 1997 season. Arizona and its fellow expansion team, the Tampa Bay Devil Rays, took turns selecting players who went unprotected by other MLB teams. The D-Backs' first pick was left-handed pitcher Brian Anderson from Cleveland. He would be a regular part of Arizona's starting rotation for the next five seasons. They also landed lefty Omar Daal, who won 24 games over the Diamondbacks' first two seasons. Outfielder David Dellucci, catchers Kelly Stinnett and Damian Miller, and infielder Hanley Frias also arrived from

Matt Williams makes an off-balance throw trying to get the out from third base in a 1998 game against the Oakland Athletics.

the expansion draft and made important contributions in the team's first few seasons.

The expansion draft also produced one huge part of the Diamondbacks' immediate future. After the draft, Arizona made a series of trades that ended with the team gaining third baseman Matt Williams. The right-handed power hitter had starred for the San Francisco Giants throughout the 1990s. Williams went on to spend the final six years of his career with the Diamondbacks.

That first season, however, was a rough one. Like most expansion teams, the D-Backs struggled with their collection of cast-offs and youngsters. Their team batting average was the worst in the NL, and their pitching staff struck out the fewest batters in the league.

Rookie first baseman Travis Lee and veteran center fielder Devon White tied for the team lead with 22 home runs. White's .279 batting average was the best among the team's regulars. Williams, a four-time All-Star during his time with the Giants, provided veteran leadership. Right-hander Andy Benes, who signed as a free agent just before spring training, led the pitching staff with 14 wins.

The 1998 Diamondbacks limped out of the gate, winning just two of their first 15 games. An eight-game losing streak in early May ended any dreams of a winning season. Though a seven-game winning streak that started in late August provided a glimmer of hope. In the end, the first-year D-Backs posted a 65–97 record, finishing dead last in the NL West. Little did the baseball world know that the team in the desert was about to launch a historic turnaround the next year.

CHAPTER 2

DESERT POWER

Expansion teams are expected to struggle. But Jerry Colangelo was not a patient man. He was used to success. In his early days as an NBA executive, he'd overseen the Phoenix Suns' surprise run to the NBA Finals in just their eighth year of existence.

MLB had its own recent model to follow for quick turnarounds. The Florida Marlins began play in 1993. They won the World Series in 1997. If the Marlins could go from the basement to the top of the baseball world in their fifth season, Colangelo reasoned, why couldn't his Diamondbacks do the same?

Randy Johnson led the league in strikeouts in five of his eight seasons with the Diamondbacks.

In 1999 many of the team's top players from the previous year were back. But Arizona made several key offseason pickups. The biggest one, Randy Johnson, stood 6-foot-10. Nicknamed "the Big Unit" this left-hander was one of the most intimidating pitchers in the game. He helped build the Seattle Mariners into a playoff team with his blazing fastball. Johnson led the American League (AL) in strikeouts for four straight seasons. In 1998 he led the majors with 329 strikeouts. He was traded from Seattle to the Houston Astros during the season. And he went 10–1 to help the Astros win their division.

After the season, the 35-year-old Johnson became a free agent. And he had plenty of teams that wanted to sign him. He chose Arizona because he lived in a suburb of Phoenix and liked the team's potential. The Diamondbacks had already added free agent pitchers Todd Stottlemyre and Armando

HAVING A BLAST

The Diamondbacks' pitching was great in 1999. But the team's offensive improvement was the key to the season. Luis Gonzalez (26) and Steve Finley (34) combined for 60 homers. But infielders Matt Williams and Jay Bell, holdovers from the first season, led the way. Bell blasted 38 homers and drove in 112 runs. Williams finished with 35 home runs and 142 runs batted in (RBIs). The D-Backs led the NL in runs scored and finished second in home runs and triples.

Diamondbacks slugger Steve Finley bats against the Los Angeles Dodgers in a 1999 game.

Travis Lee placed third in Rookie of the Year voting during his debut season with the Diamondbacks.

Reynoso to improve the rotation. Along with Andy Benes, Omar Daal, and Brian Anderson, the D-Backs were suddenly loaded with quality starting pitchers.

The team's hitting still needed improvement, though. Two new outfielders helped support those concerns. Colangelo signed free agent center fielder Steve Finley from the San Diego Padres. Finley had made the NL All-Star team two years earlier. At age 34, he was thought by many to be past his prime. Finley proved his doubters wrong. He hit 34 homers and drove in 103 runs in his first year with the D-Backs.

Finally, a seemingly minor trade turned out to be one of the most important moves in team history. In late December, Arizona sent outfielder Karim García to the Detroit Tigers for outfielder Luis Gonzalez. Arizona had acquired García in the expansion draft and stuck with him through a shaky first season before deciding to move on from him.

Meanwhile, Gonzalez had bounced around to three teams in his first nine major league seasons. A career .268 hitter with moderate power, Gonzalez was expected to give the Diamondbacks consistent, if not flashy, play in left field. Like Finley, Gonzalez thrived in the desert. In 1999 the 31-year-old Gonzalez played in his first All-Star Game and posted career-best stats with a .336 batting average, 26 home runs, and 111 runs batted in (RBIs).

Johnson pitches a shutout against the San Diego Padres in the 1999 season. He only allowed six hits and struck out 12 batters in the 4–0 win.

SURPRISE IN THE WEST

Hopes were high coming out of training camp in the spring of 1999. If the D-Backs could just avoid another rough start, maybe they could build some momentum and grab an early lead in the division race.

Instead, the Diamondbacks lost five of their first six games, all on the road. The Los Angeles Dodgers swept a three-game series, with two of the wins coming in extra innings. Then the D-Backs flew to Atlanta and lost two of three to the Braves. They suffered two more walk-off defeats in the process.

But this team was too talented to sputter for a second straight season. The Diamondbacks returned to Phoenix and pounded the Dodgers in their home opener. A grand slam by Travis Lee led the way to a 12–6 win. The next night, the D-Backs rallied for three runs in the 16th inning to pull out a 7–6 thriller. And with that, they were on their way. They finished with eight wins in their next 10 home games, showing the rest of the league that they were serious contenders.

By Memorial Day, the Diamondbacks had taken over first place in the NL West for the second year. And they stayed there throughout June. They tumbled to second for three weeks in July, but when Anderson threw eight scoreless innings and Finley hit his 19th homer to beat the Dodgers 3–0 on July 24, Arizona moved into first place to stay. The D-Backs clinched the division in fitting fashion with Johnson on the mound. The veteran lefty picked up his 16th win, going the distance in an 11–3 win at San Francisco.

The Diamondbacks won 10 of their final 12 games to finish the season 100–62. They opened their first postseason with a best-of-five series against the New York Mets. This was a strong Mets team that was a year away from winning the NL pennant.

The teams split the first two games in Arizona, but the Mets won the next two at home to end the D-Backs' dream season.

Still, all was not lost. Matt Williams finished third in Most Valuable Player (MVP) voting after hitting 35 homers and driving in 142 runs. Johnson went 17–9 and led the majors with 364 strikeouts. That helped him win the NL Cy Young Award, given to the best pitcher in the league. He had already won the award in the AL with Seattle in 1995. Daal nearly matched him with 16 victories, while Benes won 13 and Reynoso won 10. Closer Matt Mantei, a midseason pickup in a trade with the Marlins, saved 22 games in 25 chances.

Expectations for a repeat ran high in 2000. But Williams missed the first seven weeks of the season with a broken bone in his foot. That was the first of two injuries that limited him to just 96 games played on the season. Without Williams putting up his usual big numbers in the middle of the lineup, the offense tailed off sharply. Johnson had another good year, winning 19 games, another MLB strikeout crown, and his second straight NL Cy Young Award. But the team's record dropped to 85–77, nine games out of a playoff spot. Fortunately for Diamondbacks fans, the next turnaround was just six months away.

Diamondbacks infielder Matt Williams played for Arizona from 1998 to 2003.

ARIZONA

CHAPTER 3

WORLD CHAMPIONS

The Diamondbacks' management liked the state of their roster at the end of the 2000 season. They had a powerful lineup and two of the best starting pitchers in the game. Randy Johnson was one of them, of course. They'd picked up the other in a trade with the Phillies in July 2000. Arizona sent Omar Daal, Travis Lee, and two other players to Philadelphia in exchange for right-hander Curt Schilling. He and Johnson formed a tough one-two punch, a pair of hard-nosed veterans known for their competitive streaks.

The team's biggest change in the offseason was at manager. Owner Jerry Colangelo decided the Diamondbacks had gone as far as Buck Showalter could take them. His replacement,

Arizona's Curt Schilling pitches in a 9–2 victory against the San Francisco Giants in 2001.

Bob Brenly, was a former major league catcher and coach who had also been part of Arizona's television broadcast team.

The Diamondbacks gave the roster one minor tweak as well, adding free agent first baseman Mark Grace. The three-time All-Star had been a fixture in the Chicago Cubs' starting lineup for 13 years. Grace was a career .300 hitter who drew a lot of walks and played solid defense.

He proved to be a natural fit in the Diamondbacks' veteran-laden clubhouse. All eight position players in their regular lineup were at least 31 years old. Meanwhile, Johnson (37) and Schilling (34) anchored an experienced starting rotation.

The NL West provided plenty of competition in 2001. The San Francisco Giants and Los Angeles Dodgers were both pushing for a playoff spot. But the Diamondbacks held them off, winning the division by two games over San Francisco. Luis Gonzalez carried much of the offensive burden, posting mind-boggling numbers that season. He hit .325 with 57 home runs and 142 RBIs. But the lineup was filled with players making key contributions. Right fielder Reggie Sanders smacked 33 homers. Shortstop Tony Womack stole 28 bases. Grace posted a .386 on-base percentage.

On the mound, the D-Backs' pair of aces were as good as advertised. Schilling went 22–6, leading the majors in

Slugger Luis Gonzalez watches his second homer of the day sail out of the stadium on Opening Day against the Colorado Rockies in 2004.

victories and innings pitched. Johnson went 21–6 and led the big leagues with a 2.49 earned-run average (ERA) and 372 strikeouts. The duo finished first and second in the NL Cy Young voting, with Johnson winning for the third straight season.

POSTSEASON PRESSURE

The Diamondbacks were in the playoffs for the second time in three years. But this time around, they had some experience under their belts. They faced the St. Louis Cardinals in the NLDS. The series came down to a decisive fifth game. Schilling squared off against St. Louis ace Matt Morris. Sanders homered in the fourth inning to put the D-Backs on top 1–0. But with two outs in the eighth, Schilling gave up a solo homer to J. D. Drew to tie the game. In the top of the ninth, the Cardinals advanced a runner to second base with one out. Schilling struck out the next two hitters to end the scoring threat.

The Diamondbacks fans were tense but hopeful as the bottom of the ninth unfolded. Their faith was rewarded when Womack came to bat with Danny Bautista on second and two out. Womack lofted a soft line drive over the shortstop and into left field. Bautista raced around third and slid head-first across home plate before the throw arrived. The Diamondbacks had a dramatic 2–1 win and their first playoff series victory.

Compared with their battle against the Cardinals, the NL Championship Series (NLCS) was a breeze. Johnson won two games, Schilling had another complete-game victory, and Arizona took down the Atlanta Braves four games to one. In just their fourth season, the Diamondbacks had reached the World Series.

Their opponents were much more experienced. The New York Yankees had won more World Series titles than any other MLB team. In 2000 they beat the Mets for their third title in a row and fourth in five seasons. The Diamondbacks knew they would be facing their toughest challenge yet.

The series began in Phoenix, and the D-Backs' aces got them off to a fast start. First, Schilling tossed seven strong innings in a 9–1 win. Then Johnson struck out 11 batters as he blanked the Yankees 4–0.

SYMPATHETIC OPPONENT

The Yankees had sentiment on their side when they faced the Diamondbacks in the World Series. On September 11, 2001, terrorists attacked the United States. The twin towers at New York City's World Trade Center were reduced to rubble. The entire country rallied to support New Yorkers in the wake of the crisis.

The series shifted to New York. And that was just what the Yankees needed. They pulled out a 2–1 victory in Game 3. Then the drama went up a notch. In the ninth inning of Game 4,

Yankees first baseman Tino Martinez hit a two-run homer off Arizona closer Byung-Hyun Kim with two outs to tie the score 3–3. In the bottom of the 10th, shortstop Derek Jeter homered off Kim to win it for the Yankees and even the series.

The next night, the Diamondbacks took a 2–0 lead into the ninth inning. Brenly showed confidence in Kim and sent him out to close the game. Once again he retired two of the first three hitters. And once again, a Yankees veteran—this time, third baseman Scott Brosius—hit a two-out, two-run homer to tie the game. New York scored again in the 12th inning to win the game and send the series back to Arizona leading three games to two.

Still stinging from those three tough losses, the D-Backs took out their frustration on Yankees pitchers in Game 6. They smashed 22 hits while Johnson silenced the Yankee bats in a 15–2 thrashing. That set up a Game 7 few fans will ever forget.

Schilling was tough, but New York touched him for single runs in the seventh and eighth to take a 2–1 lead. Now the Diamondbacks had to score a run against the toughest postseason reliever of all time, Mariano Rivera. The Yankees' closer had converted 23 straight save opportunities in the playoffs and World Series. Rivera retired the D-Backs in the eighth. Johnson came out of the bullpen on no rest to keep the Yankees in check. But Arizona was down to its last three outs.

Diamondbacks first baseman Mark Grace makes an out while leaning into the crowd during Game 7 of the 2001 World Series.

Diamondbacks players celebrate their 2001 World Series championship over the New York Yankees.

Diamondbacks fans came to their feet in support of their team. A season's worth of tension and excitement had reached its peak. Grace led off the ninth with a single. Miller laid down a sacrifice bunt, and Rivera threw wildly to second. That put runners on first and second with nobody out. The roar at Bank One Ballpark was booming. Bell came up next. He bunted back to Rivera too, but this time the throw to third base was on target for the first out.

Then Womack played postseason hero again. He slashed a double down the right-field line. The tying run scored. Bell stopped at third. Craig Counsell was hit by a pitch to load the bases. That brought up Gonzalez. And Arizona's best hitter delivered. Though he got jammed by the pitch, Gonzalez was able to muscle it out into short center field for a single. He raced to first base, arms raised, as Bell ran home with the winning run. The Diamondbacks were world champions.

HARD TO REPEAT

The Diamondbacks discovered in the coming years just how special those first few years were. That's because they found their success difficult to repeat. The team did win its third NL West title in 2002, and Johnson won his fourth straight NL Cy Young Award. But the Cardinals got revenge in a three-game sweep in the first round of the playoffs.

Arizona slipped to third place in 2003, as Johnson and Schilling finally began showing their age. And then the bottom dropped out. Schilling left before the 2004 season, and Brenly was fired midway through it as the Diamondbacks lost a franchise-record 111 games. Johnson did throw a perfect game against the Braves in Atlanta on May 18, but he was traded to the Yankees after the season. By the 2006 season, only Gonzalez, Counsell, and pitcher Miguel Batista remained from the World Series team. The championship era was over. Arizona fans hoped a new one would soon begin.

Veteran stars Randy Johnson, *left*, and Curt Schilling, *right*, celebrate their 2001 World Series championship with the team trophy and the World Series MVP trophy, which was awarded to both pitchers.

Arizona

CHAPTER 4

NEW FACES, NEW ACES

Perhaps trying to bring back that championship feeling, the Diamondbacks began 2007 by getting Randy Johnson back from the New York Yankees. His veteran leadership was a big benefit on a team with many young players. Johnson pitched well for two months. But he injured his back in late June and missed the rest of the season.

By then, the Diamondbacks had a new ace atop their rotation. Right-hander Brandon Webb had made his debut with the team in 2003. He quickly became a reliable workhorse, averaging nearly 34 starts and 224 innings pitched over the next three seasons. He worked through some control issues, having led the majors in walks while suffering an NL-high

Diamondbacks starting pitcher Brandon Webb led the league in shutouts in both the 2006 and 2007 seasons.

16 losses in 2004. By 2006 Webb had turned it around, earning his first All-Star spot and leading the league with 16 victories. He also won the NL Cy Young Award, following in Johnson's footsteps to become the league's best pitcher.

Webb was even better in 2007, going 18–10 with a 3.01 ERA. He was especially tough down the stretch, winning 10 of his last 13 starts as the Diamondbacks surged to another division title. Veterans Doug Davis and Liván Hernández combined for 24 wins, and closer José Valverde led the majors with 47 saves. Bob Melvin was named NL Manager of the Year in his third season leading the Diamondbacks.

Arizona opened the postseason with a three-game sweep of the Chicago Cubs in the NLDS. But the red-hot Colorado Rockies had won 17 of their previous 18 games and were too much to handle. Colorado swept four straight from the Diamondbacks in the NLCS.

The D-Backs slipped to second place in 2008. But Webb was excellent again, winning a league-high 22 games. He began the season with nine straight victories, made his third straight All-Star Game, and finished second in the NL Cy Young voting for the second year in a row. However, starting at least 33 games in each of five straight years finally caught up with Webb. He started the 2009 season opener but was soon placed on the disabled list with a right shoulder injury.

Justin Upton makes a diving catch against the Atlanta Braves in 2007.

First baseman Paul Goldschmidt gets a hit against the Atlanta Braves in his rookie season with the Diamondbacks in 2011.

Despite surgery and extensive rehab, Webb never pitched in the majors again.

Missing their ace, the D-Backs tumbled into last place in 2009 and stayed there in 2010. But a rebuilt rotation helped push them back to the top of the NL West in 2011. Ian Kennedy, a 26-year-old right-hander, went 21–4. Two other young starters, Daniel Hudson (age 24) and Josh Collmenter (age 25), combined for 26 victories. And new closer J. J. Putz posted 45 saves to lead a deep and talented bullpen.

The pitching had to be good. Because unlike the great Diamondbacks teams of a decade earlier, their hitting was somewhat limited. Just 23 years old, right fielder Justin Upton made his second All-Star Game and finished with 31 homers. Catcher Miguel Montero was also an All-Star and drove in 86 runs. But their lack of offense finally bit them in the NLDS when they lost to the Milwaukee Brewers in five games. The D-Backs scored just seven runs in three games at Milwaukee, finally suffering a 3–2 loss in Game 5 in 10 innings.

KIRK GIBSON

The D-Backs hired former Tigers and Dodgers great Kirk Gibson as their manager midway through the 2010 season. In his first full year in charge, Gibson led Arizona to 94 wins and the NL West title. He was rewarded for his efforts with the NL Manager of the Year Award.

GOLDY'S GANG

The 2011 season included the debut of Arizona's next big star. Paul Goldschmidt took over at first base the last two months. He remained a fixture there for the next seven seasons. The right-handed slugger hit for average and power.

Arizona center fielder Ketel Marte led the majors in triples (12) in 2018.

Goldschmidt led the NL with 36 homers and 125 RBIs in 2013, the first of his six straight All-Star seasons.

The D-Backs had a hard time putting talent around Goldschmidt. They had a few success stories, though. Center fielder A. J. Pollock emerged as a starter in 2013 and was an All-Star in 2015 when he stole 39 bases and hit .315. Jake Lamb took over third base in 2015 and hit 59 homers over the next two seasons. Flame-throwing right-hander Zack Greinke arrived in 2016 and averaged 15 wins over the next three seasons.

By 2017 Arizona was finally ready to compete for the postseason under first-year manager Torey Lovullo. Goldschmidt led the way at the plate with 36 homers and 120 RBIs. Greinke went 17–7, while young lefties Patrick Corbin and Robbie Ray combined for 29 wins. And in July, the team traded three minor leaguers to Detroit for outfielder J. D. Martinez. He hit 29 homers the rest of the way, including four in a game at Dodger Stadium on September 4. The Diamondbacks finished 11 games behind Los Angeles in the West. But their 93–69 record was good enough to clinch home field in the NL wild-card game. There they defeated the Rockies 11–8, with Pollock's two-run triple sealing the win. However, the Dodgers swept them in the NLDS.

Goldschmidt stuck around for one more season before he was traded to the St. Louis Cardinals in exchange for three other players in December 2018. Center fielder Ketel Marte emerged as the new team leader, hitting .329 with 32 homers and making his first All-Star Game. But the Diamondbacks quickly fell to the bottom of the West, losing 110 games in 2021. Going forward, Arizona fans hoped Marte, catcher/outfielder Daulton Varsho, and young pitchers Zac Gallen and Merrill Kelly could form the heart of the next great Diamondbacks team.

TIMELINE

1995

In March, Phoenix, Arizona, is granted an expansion franchise by MLB. The team is set to begin play in 1998.

1995

Jerry Colangelo, owner of the new Arizona Diamondbacks, hires Buck Showalter as the team's first manager in November.

1998

The Diamondbacks go 65–97 in their first season.

1999

Arizona makes the playoffs in just its second season, winning 100 games and the NL West title before falling to the Mets in the NLDS.

2001

The Diamondbacks beat the Yankees in seven dramatic games to win the World Series.

2002

Lefty Randy Johnson wins his fourth straight NL Cy Young Award.

2004

Johnson throws a perfect game at Atlanta on May 18 and wins his ninth MLB strikeout crown, but manager Bob Brenly is fired in the middle of a 111-loss season.

2007

With the help of 2006 NL Cy Young winner Brandon Webb, manager Bob Melvin guides the D-Backs to 90 wins and the NL West title.

2008

In his second stint with the team, Johnson goes 11–10 as the Diamondbacks fall two games short of the playoffs at 82–80.

2011

Kirk Gibson leads the Diamondbacks to 94 wins and the NL West crown in his first full season as manager.

2013

Paul Goldschmidt leads the NL with 36 home runs and 125 RBIs and earns the first of six straight All-Star Game nods.

2017

The Diamondbacks win the NL wild-card game over the Rockies 11–8 before being swept by the Dodgers in the NLDS.

2019

Goldschmidt is traded by the Diamondbacks to the Cardinals in December 2018.

2021

The bottom drops out again as the Diamondbacks lose 110 games.

TEAM FACTS

FRANCHISE HISTORY

Arizona Diamondbacks (1998–)

WORLD SERIES CHAMPIONSHIPS

2001

KEY PLAYERS

Jay Bell (1998–2002)
Steve Finley (1999–2004)
Paul Goldschmidt (2011–18)
Luis Gonzalez (1999–2006)
Zack Greinke (2016–19)
Randy Johnson (1999–04, 2007–08)
Ketel Marte (2017–)
David Peralta (2014–)
A. J. Pollock (2012–18)
Curt Schilling (2000–03)
Justin Upton (2007–12)
Brandon Webb (2003–09)

KEY MANAGERS

Bob Brenly (2001–04)
Kirk Gibson (2010–14)
Torey Lovullo (2017–)
Bob Melvin (2005–09)
Buck Showalter (1998–2000)

HOME STADIUMS

Bank One Ballpark (1998–2005)
Chase Field (2006–)

TEAM TRIVIA

FAST LEARNERS

No MLB expansion team has won a league championship in less time than the four years it took the Diamondbacks to win the World Series.

HANDCUFFING HITTERS

Besides Randy Johnson's perfect game, two other Arizona pitchers have thrown no-hitters through 2021: Edwin Jackson (2010) and Tyler Gilbert (2021).

CIRCLE THE BASES

Second baseman Aaron Hill hit for the cycle twice in 12 days in June 2012. A cycle is when a batter hits a single, a double, a triple, and a home run in the same game. Only four other Diamondbacks had hit for the cycle through 2021.

SEEING RED

The team's primary colors were purple and teal through 2006. The next year they changed to a new look, with red and black as their main colors.

SPLASH!

Bank One Ballpark, now known as Chase Field, has a swimming pool beyond the outfield fence. Mark Grace hit the first home run into the pool in 1998, when he was playing for the Chicago Cubs.

GLOSSARY

ace

A team's best starting pitcher.

bullpen

The place where relief pitchers warm up; also used to refer to a team's relievers as a group.

closer

A pitcher who comes in at the end of the game to secure a win for his team.

expansion team

A brand-new team brought into an existing league.

free agent

A player whose rights are not owned by any team.

no-hitter

A complete game in which a team does not allow any hits.

on-base percentage

A measure of a player's ability to reach base via a hit, a walk, or being hit by a pitch.

pennant

Another name for a league championship; in MLB, refers to winning either the American or National League.

perfect game

A complete game in which no batter reaches base.

sweep

Winning every game in a series.

veteran

A player who has played for many years.

walk-off defeat

A win for the home team in the final inning, forcing the defense to walk off the field.

MORE INFORMATION

BOOKS

Flynn, Brendan. *The MLB Encyclopedia*. Minneapolis, MN: Abdo Publishing, 2022.

Gitlin, Marty. *MLB*. Minneapolis, MN: Abdo Publishing, 2021.

Mitchell, Bo. *Ultimate MLB Road Trip*. Minneapolis, MN: Abdo Publishing, 2019.

ONLINE RESOURCES

To learn more about the Arizona Diamondbacks, please visit **abdobooklinks.com** or scan this QR code. These links are routinely monitored and updated to provide the most current information available.

INDEX

ABOUT THE AUTHOR

Patrick Donnelly is a freelance writer who lives in Minneapolis, Minnesota. He has covered Major League Baseball for more than 20 years.